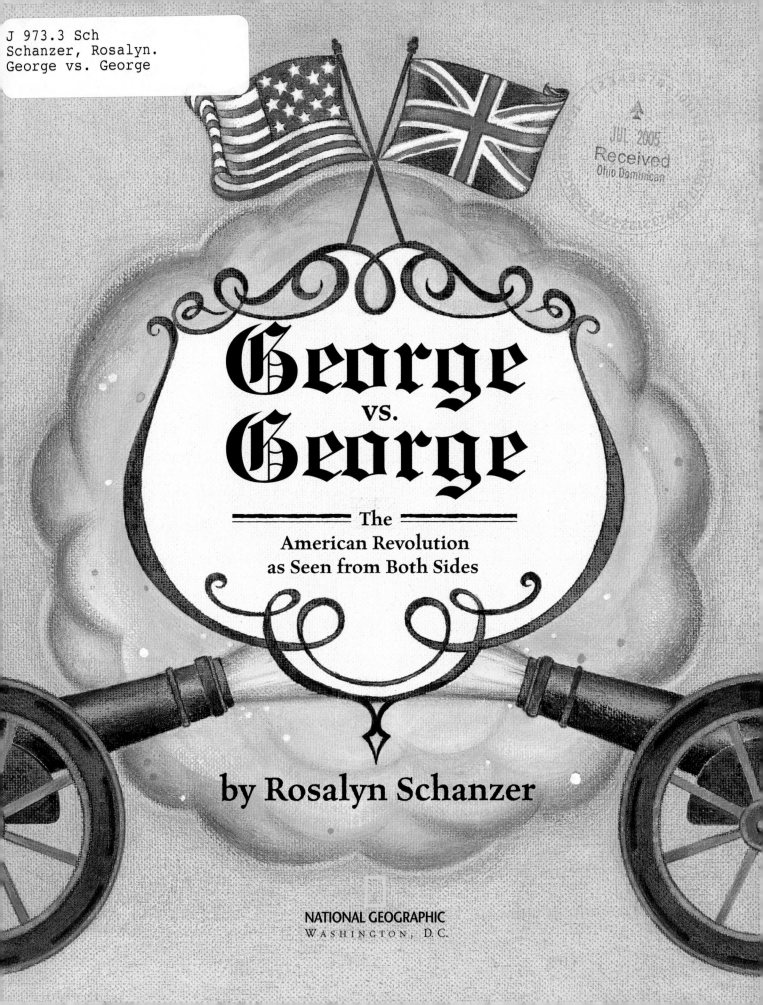

George vs. George

The

American Revolution as Seen from Both Sides

by Rosalyn Schanzer

NATIONAL GEOGRAPHIC
WASHINGTON, D.C.

For Nancy, JaneE, and Steve

Printed in Belgium

Library of Congress Cataloging-in-Publication Data

Schanzer, Rosalyn.
George vs. George : the American Revolution as seen from both sides / by Rosalyn
Schanzer.
p. cm.
Summary: Explores how the characters and lives of King George III
of England and George Washington affected the progress and outcome
of the American Revolution.
Includes bibliographical references.
1. United States—History—Revolution, 1775–1783—Juvenile literature.
2. Washington, George, 1732–1799—Juvenile literature. 3. George III, King of Great
Britain, 1738–1820—Juvenile literature. 4. Presidents—United
States—Biography—Juvenile literature. 5. Generals—United
States—Biography—Juvenile literature. 6. Great Britain—Kings and
rulers—Biography—Juvenile literature. 7. United States—History—Colonial period,
ca. 1600–1775—Juvenile literature. 8. Great Britain—History—George III,
1760–1820—Juvenile literature. [1. United States—History—Revolution, 1775–1783.
2. Washington, George, 1732–1799. 3. Presidents. 4. George III, King of Great
Britain, 1738–1820. 5. Kings, queens, rulers, etc. 6. Great Britain—History—
George III, 1760–1820.] I. Title.
E209.S33 2004
973.3–dc22   2003020843

All of the speech balloons in this book contain real quotes from real people. To see where I found these quotes, look in the back of the book.

THE AUTHOR

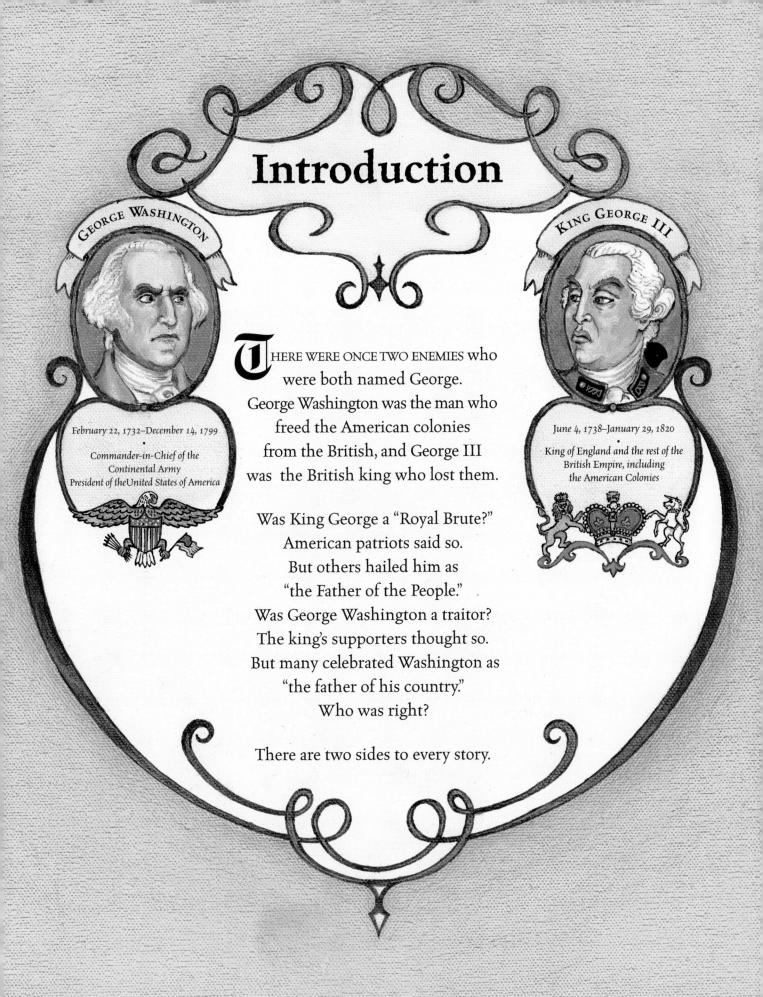

Introduction

GEORGE WASHINGTON

February 22, 1732–December 14, 1799
•
Commander-in-Chief of the
Continental Army
President of the United States of America

KING GEORGE III

June 4, 1738–January 29, 1820
•
King of England and the rest of the
British Empire, including
the American Colonies

THERE WERE ONCE TWO ENEMIES who
were both named George.
George Washington was the man who
freed the American colonies
from the British, and George III
was the British king who lost them.

Was King George a "Royal Brute?"
American patriots said so.
But others hailed him as
"the Father of the People."
Was George Washington a traitor?
The king's supporters thought so.
But many celebrated Washington as
"the father of his country."
Who was right?

There are two sides to every story.

At First Glance

The year was 1763, and in many ways, George Washington of America and King George III of Great Britain were very much alike. Both men had light blue eyes and reddish-brown hair.* Athletic and dignified in appearance, each stood well over 6 feet tall, towering above most other men during a time when the average height was 5'7". Both were honest and popular with the public. They liked simple food and

GEORGE WASHINGTON

Mark yon tall and daring warrior...a people yet unborn will hail him as the founder of a mighty empire.

INDIAN CHIEF
Fought against George Washington in 1755

*King George usually wore a white wig, which was the height of fashion in those days. George Washington sometimes powdered his hair to make it look white.

much preferred plain clothes to the high-fashion outfits of the period decorated with lace, ruffles, and embroidery.

George III was sometimes called "farmer George" because of his life-long interest in agriculture. George Washington *was* a farmer who was happiest when working on his land. Both were excellent horsemen and loved hunting. George III believed that a king should rule America. For a long time, George Washington thought so, too. He had even fought bravely alongside the British Army.

KING GEORGE

Of him we are much inclined to hope great things.

SAMUEL JOHNSON
Greatest English writer of his day

The people of Great Britain and the people from Britain's American colonies had a lot in common, too. Most everyone on both sides of the ocean liked their good-natured young "Patriot King." English was their main language; after all, 60 percent of the colonists had British ancestors. London was everybody's capital city, and many Americans proudly thought of England as "home."

Great Britain had just won the Seven Years War*, which involved almost every country in Europe and extended all the way to India and Australia. King George was now the ruler of the world's greatest empire. As loyal citizens of Great Britain, colonial soldiers had joined forces with soldiers from England to fight against France for control of North America. When France gave up its territories, jubilant

*The part of the Seven Years War fought in North America is called the French and Indian War.

celebrations were held throughout both England and America.

Who could imagine that the fabric binding America to Great Britain was about to unravel or that the two Georges were about to become bitter enemies? Who could guess that George III would be the last king of America, and that George Washington would one day become its first president?

Neither George Washington nor King George III was fully responsible for everything that happened next. Many other thinkers, soldiers, and politicians helped to shape the future. Even so, as leaders of the two sides, these two Georges were to become the strongest symbols of their countries during the next 20 years. The different ideas they stood for would soon turn the whole world upside-down.

BRITANNIA RULE THE WAVES!
Patriotic song written by James Thomson — mid 18th century

OCEAN

GREAT BRITAIN

A Look at the Life of
King George & His Countrymen

George III was 22 years old when he succeeded his grandfather as king in 1760. He was married to a German princess named Charlotte, and they would become the parents of 15 children. The king was absolutely devoted to his family.

Their favorite home was a palace in the English countryside surrounded by roses, pinks, carnations, and orange, lemon, and tea trees. But they spent most of their time in a smaller red brick mansion called Buckingham House (usually known as the Queen's House) in London, England, the capital of Great Britain, where the king worked.

London, with its 740,000 inhabitants, was the biggest city in Europe and the center of British government. London's residents were proud of their long history and high level of cultural achievement. For fun, they went to masked balls and the theater, gambled at cards, dice, and roulette, belonged to all sorts of clubs, and met at coffeehouses, taverns, cockfights, chophouses, and pleasure gardens. Noisy streets teemed with horses, carriages, ballad singers, flower-sellers, fishmongers, and ladies and gentlemen in fancy white wigs wearing all the latest fashions.

But the overcrowded city had its share of problems, too. The death rate was high. All the coal that residents used as fuel caused black rain and thick, sooty smog. Food and drinking water were often unhealthy, riots were common, and public hangings drew rowdy mobs. Thousands of beggars and pickpockets were evidence of poverty run amok.

Enormous crowds from all classes flocked to watch summer concerts in London's 15 pleasure gardens.

Great Britain

■ British possessions in 1763

The English were convinced that the rest of the British Empire was backward and uncivilized. King George ruled 31 colonies and other possessions in many parts of the world, from Borneo to the Bay of Bengal, and all the way to Honduras. Throughout England, people argued constantly about world politics, but they would soon argue especially hard about the uprising over in America.

A Look at the Life of
George Washingon & His Countrymen

George Washington was married to a wealthy widow named Martha Custis. Tiny, outgoing, and plump, Martha was a charming hostess. More than 2,000 guests visited their Mount Vernon home in the years before 1775. Martha had two young children from her previous marriage, and Washington adored them.

The couple enlarged Mount Vernon into an enormous self-contained community. Washington grew tobacco, then switched to wheat. Besides raising mules, sheep, hogs, and prize bulls, he also bred horses and fox-hounds, netted tons of fish, and grew such things as wild grapes, Indian corn, oats, clover, flax, hemp, and nut, apple, pear, apricot, and cherry trees. He even grew orange trees that spent the winter in his greenhouse. Gardeners, shoemakers, blacksmiths, weavers, foremen, and sometimes Washington's nieces and nephews all lived on the estate. Like all other plantation owners at the time, Washington was a slave owner. By 1775, he owned 135 people.

The Thirteen Colonies in 1763

About 90 percent of the colonists in America lived out in the country, where new arrivals from Europe were amazed to find farm land, forests, fish, and game as far as the eye could see. So much fertile territory made it possible to supply Great Britain with raw goods such as furs, flour, iron, tobacco, and lumber in return for manufactured goods, including cloth, shoes, furniture, and tea from Great Britain.

In small but bustling port cities such as Philadelphia, New York, Boston, and Charleston, whaling and shipbuilding were already major industries. And there were lumber mills, flourmills, factories, firehouses, and colleges. Streets—some paved, most full of mud or dust—overflowed with oxcarts, horses and carriages, chimney sweeps, sailors, and carriers of wood. In local taverns, young girls danced lively jigs with their boyfriends.

The most well-off, best-educated people were usually planters (like George Washington), merchants, doctors, ministers, or lawyers. Next came a very large middle class that included small farmers, shopkeepers, teachers, craftsmen, and fishermen. The poorest were unskilled laborers, indentured servants, and, of course, black slaves from Africa who were bought, sold, and held in bondage in all 13 of the colonies.

Many colonists wanted to settle the new territory they had helped to win during the Seven Years War, but Great Britain made it illegal. London thought it was fairest and safest to reserve these lands for the Native Americans who had always lived and hunted there. George Washington agreed with plenty of other colonial settlers, who thought the law unfairly limited their rights. They poured into the west anyway.

How Government Worked in England

The British government was a constitutional monarchy, which was a fancy way of saying that King George did not have all the power. He and a governing body called Parliament worked together to rule the Empire. Young King George tried hard—and with much success—to see that Parliament's decisions agreed with his point of view. Even so, he had some very strong opponents, and it was Parliament that made laws and controlled the purse strings.

King George III

British Parliament
(governing body with two houses)

House of Lords
(upper house)

Made up of noblemen who
inherited the right to be members.

House of Commons
(lower house)

Members were elected by the people,
but sons of noblemen often rigged their own
elections or bought their seats.

Voters

Fewer than one in five men were allowed to vote in England,
and these men usually had to own land or businesses for the privilege.

How Government Worked in America

The 13 American colonies were not yet united into a single country. Each separate colony was under the Crown's control, and each had its own governor and a governing body that made laws and imposed taxes. Some people who served in the government were elected by colonists. For example, George Washington was an elected member of the Virginia House of Burgesses (the lower house). For years England had looked the other way when colonists ignored British laws they didn't like.

King George III   **British Parliament**

13 Governors

Each colony had its own governor. All but 2 were appointed by the Crown to serve as Great Britain's chief representatives. Their job was to enforce British laws and carry out British orders.

13 Governing Bodies

Made laws for each colony and sent them to England for approval. Like the British Parliament, most governing bodies had two houses:

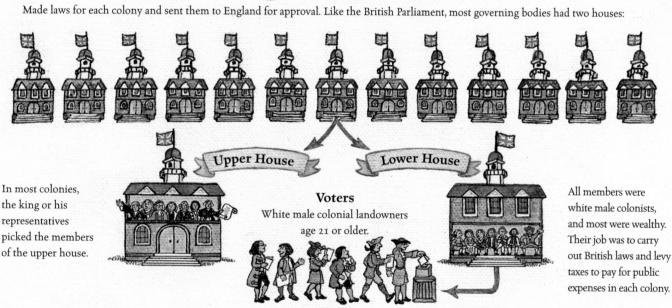

Upper House   **Lower House**

In most colonies, the king or his representatives picked the members of the upper house.

Voters
White male colonial landowners age 21 or older.

All members were white male colonists, and most were wealthy. Their job was to carry out British laws and levy taxes to pay for public expenses in each colony.

The Trouble with Taxes
1764–1770

So what stirred up the hornet's nest in the first place? It all began over money—and over the rights of citizens, too. Great Britain had been in one war or another for 50 years and was drowning in debt. Over in London, Parliament decided that Americans should help out by paying their fair share, and King George agreed. After all, Great Britain had spent plenty of money fighting in America for the good of the colonies. The crown was still supporting a British Army to help stop Indian attacks on the American frontier. It was Great Britain's right to collect payment!

To raise the money, Parliament passed a Sugar Act and a Stamp Act saying that colonists had to pay taxes to Great Britain for all sorts of imported goods, from molasses, blue indigo dye, and pimentos to printed items such as marriage licenses, playing cards, and newspapers. Similar taxes were often collected in England. But the colonists were already paying separate taxes to cover their own war debts and to run the colonies. A lot of them thought paying twice wasn't one bit fair. Besides, they believed it was against the British Constitution.

Ever since the Middle Ages, English law had said that there should be "no taxation without representation." This meant that citizens could never be taxed unless their elected representatives voted to pay. The colonists were British citizens, and the law guaranteed them the "rights of Englishmen." So where was their right to have representatives who could vote for or against these taxes? Though many colonists would stay loyal to the crown and obey its laws no matter what, others argued that Parliament might make them pay even more taxes without their consent.

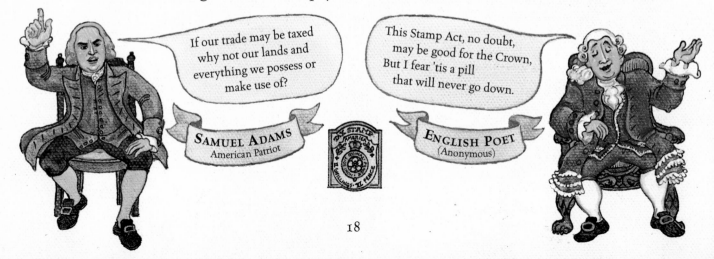

If our trade may be taxed why not our lands and everything we possess or make use of?

SAMUEL ADAMS
American Patriot

This Stamp Act, no doubt, may be good for the Crown, But I fear 'tis a pill that will never go down.

ENGLISH POET
(Anonymous)

Many colonial merchants refused to buy British goods. Pamphlet writers roared. Preachers thundered from their pulpits. Angry members of an organization called the Sons of Liberty stripped royal office holders naked and covered them with hot tar and goose feathers. (They used to tar-and-feather folks in Great Britain, too, in those days.)

A mob completely wrecked the home of the Royal Governor of Massachusetts. A straw dummy dressed to look like a stamp distributor was hung from a 120-year-old elm tree, and the British tax stamps that Americans were supposed to buy were burned in every colony.

CHARLES TOWNSHEND
Treasurer of Parliament

By the time the Stamp Act was supposed to go into effect in November of 1765, flags were being flown at half-mast to mourn the death of liberty. Nobody in America would even distribute the stamps.

Four months later, hoping to restore peace, Parliament finally gave up and got rid of the hated taxes. This troubled King George, who still thought the taxes were fair, but he signed the repeal anyway. British merchants were delighted to get their lost customers back, and all of America celebrated.

Well, the story could have ended right there, but of course it didn't. To show they weren't afraid to tax the colonies, Parliament started demanding even more taxes. Patriot leaders in Massachusetts and Virginia made polite protests to the king, but politeness didn't help one bit.

King George believed that God gave noblemen the divine right to rule and that the colonists had a duty to obey. The British stubbornly informed legislatures in both colonies that they couldn't have any more meetings. So the colonists stopped trying to be polite. The Virginians (including George Washington) met anyway and banned the sale of all items taxed by Great Britain.

Colonists smuggled in untaxed goods from other countries, which was illegal. And they made lots of their own goods instead of buying British ones. A women's group called the Daughters of Liberty supported the cause by weaving their own cloth, making their own ball gowns, and brewing their own liberty tea out of sassafras flowers.

King George was sure that certain "gentlemen who pretend to be patriots" in Massachusetts were no more than criminals, so he sent a fleet of warships to Boston to make them behave. Seven hundred soldiers wearing fancy uniforms soon paraded up Boston's streets with muskets on their shoulders. Whenever they went off duty, many stole, got drunk, and chased women. Some also infuriated worshipers by purposely racing horses, beating drums, and gambling under church windows on Sundays.

In March 1770, an angry mob of American rowdies started taunting eight of King George's soldiers and pelting them with icy snowballs. Then someone threw a lump of wood at a redcoat and knocked him flat. The enraged troops began firing into the crowd, and five colonists were killed. Furious Sons of Liberty were quick to label this disaster "the Boston Massacre," and it stirred up plenty of anger on both sides.*

* Even so, an American jury later acquitted the British commanding officer and six of his men in a fair trial. Two others were branded on their thumbs and dismissed from the army.

22

A Tempest Over Tea
1770–1774

There must always be one tax to keep up the right...As such, I approve of the Tea Duty.

KING GEORGE

It just so happened that on the very same day as the violence in Boston, Parliament and King George over in London were trying to keep the peace. They got rid of all import taxes except for one tiny tax on British tea. They thought that would solve the problem, but it didn't. Lots of colonists resented paying *any* British taxes, no matter how tiny. It was a matter of principle. Some refused to drink British tea and drank tea smuggled from Holland instead. Others, including George Washington, stopped drinking tea altogether.

By 1773, the British East India Company had so much unsold tea sitting around that it was about to go broke. To keep this tea company in business, Great Britain's prime minister, Lord North, proclaimed that absolutely nobody except the East India Company could sell any tea in America. To convince colonists to buy the tea, prices were set so low that even with tea taxes, the company's tea cost less than any other tea sold in England or in America.

The colonists loved tea, but most of them still thought this was taxation without representation. British tea either rotted in warehouses or got sent straight back to England.

Before long, Royal Governor of Massachusetts Thomas Hutchinson declared that unless the tax was paid, none of the tea shipped to Boston Harbor could be sent away. If the tea was not unloaded, ship commanders would "force it on shore under the cover of their cannon's mouth."

On the night of December 16, 1773, some Sons of Liberty covered their faces and hands with coal dust, disguised themselves as Mohawk Indians, and very calmly filed on board three ships filled with tea. Hundreds gathered to watch as the men split open 342 chests of British Darjeeling tea with tomahawks and fed all 45 tons of it to the fish.

Most Britains were outraged when they heard news of the wanton destruction. Americans were clearly "a race of convicts." They had gone too far and must be punished! Six months later, the king and an angry Parliament closed Boston Harbor. Nothing could come in, and nothing could go out.

George vs. George
1774–1775

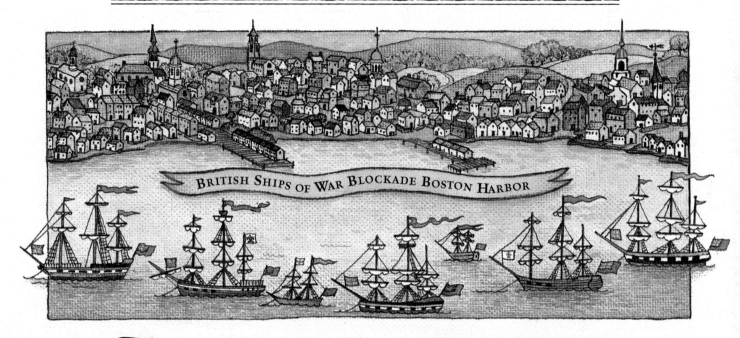

BRITISH SHIPS OF WAR BLOCKADE BOSTON HARBOR

The port closure quickly put huge numbers of Bostonians out of work. People were afraid they would starve. Other colonies scrambled to help by sending food, clothing, and flocks of sheep. Americans smuggled in at least 5,000 chests of tea from Holland alone. They also smuggled in gunpowder. Bostonians began to think of war.

As the siege continued, people from all over the colonies became more and more alarmed. If Boston was in such a sea of trouble, who was to say that worse things couldn't happen in Philadelphia or Williamsburg or Charleston? George Washington didn't approve of the Tea Party one bit, but he approved of the punishment even less.

GEORGE WASHINGTON

I am ready to raise 1,000 men, subsist them myself at my own expense, and march at their head to Boston.

During September and October of 1774, delegates from all 13 colonies met together in one place for the first time ever at the First Continental Congress in Philadelphia. George Washington was one of the delegates. The Congress sent an appeal for peace and harmony to King George and suggested that Parliament get rid of all the unconstitutional laws controlling America. Until then, the colonies would not import or buy any British goods and would not export any of their own goods to the mother country.

The Shot Heard Round the World

British General Thomas Gage had been trying hard to keep the peace in Massachusetts, but he was ordered in the name of the king to use more force. In April 1775, a spy in Boston warned Gage that colonial troublemakers were stashing big piles of ammunition in nearby Concord. This was bad news. A bloody war could break out! Gage decided that the British Army had better go seize John Hancock and Sam Adams, two rebel leaders who were hiding out in Lexington. Then they should burn the weapons in Concord before people started getting themselves killed. Gage quickly planned a secret raid.

A British regiment shivered through a chilly night rowing and then wading across the Charles River. On the morning of April 19, the soldiers had marched as far as Lexington when they came across about seventy patriot militia gathered on the village green. The rebels were armed because rebel spies William Dawes and Paul Revere had spread the alarm that the British were on their way.

> Lay down your arms, you...rebels, or you are all dead men!

JOHN PITCAIRN
British Major

LEXINGTON

Everybody's nerves were on edge. Still holding their weapons, the patriots began to back away and look for cover. Then someone fired a shot—nobody knows who—but as soon as they heard it, the British soldiers started shooting. Eight Americans were killed, and ten more were wounded. Not everyone realized it at the time, but the Revolutionary War had just begun. John Hancock and Sam Adams had disappeared. The redcoats marched on to Concord to destroy the ammunition, but most of the ammunition had vanished, too. Meanwhile, great multitudes of men from farms and villages all over the countryside gathered to fight back.

Each side told a different tale about Lexington and Concord. Rebel newspapers reported that bloodthirsty redcoats burned houses, drove naked women into the streets, and butchered old men and infants. The King was told that rebel savages broke the rules of war by ambushing his army. Then they scalped fallen British infantry and cut off their ears.

George Washington was already famous for his fearless leadership when he had fought alongside the British 20 years earlier. On June 15, 1775, the Second Continental Congress gathered in Philadelphia and unanimously elected the 43-year-old Virginian to become Commander-in-Chief of their newly formed Continental Army. But how could a small, poorly trained army with almost no money defeat one of the world's most awesome military powers? Washington refused to accept any salary, asking only that Congress pay his expenses.

I do not think myself equal to the Command.

GEORGE WASHINGTON

The very next morning, long before Washington took command of his troops, the redcoats back in Massachusetts awoke to discover an amazing sight. In just one night, about 1,200 rebels had secretly built a massive fort atop Breed's Hill* by Charlestown. Both sides fought fiercely until the rebels finally ran out of powder and ammunition. The rebels ended up losing the hill, but the British lost 92 officers, more than half their men, and more than twice as many soldiers as the rebels lost.

* *Some say that the rebels' original plan was to occupy Bunker Hill, which was higher and easier to defend. This fight came to be known as the Battle of Bunker Hill.*

British Forces

King George made it official: The colonists were rebel outlaws "misled by dangerous and ill-designing Men...traitorously preparing War." Enough was enough! He had to show them who was boss. The king enlisted more troops in Britain and hired German troops, too. He sent ships to blockade the American coast so the colonists couldn't get any outside supplies. Then his soldiers sat back to wait for the colonial army to fall to pieces. The king's war-hardened, brutally disciplined, and well-trained fighting force included five kinds of fighters.

BRITISH REGULARS
(ALSO CALLED REDCOATS)

All senior officers were noblemen. Each step up in rank was bought for large sums of money. Privates usually enlisted for life. Most were recruited in taverns, debtors' prisons, and slums, or were convicted criminals. Though their pay was extremely low, every single one proudly wore an elegant, brightly colored uniform. Officers and privates alike looked down their noses at the Americans as backward peasants who couldn't be taken seriously. To them, George Washington was a rabble-rouser, not a general. British officers addressed him as Mr. Washington instead of General Washington in their letters.

MAJOR GENERAL • LIGHT DRAGOON • GRENADIER OFFICER

LIGHT INFANTRY • PRIVATE FOOT SOLDIER • ROYAL HIGHLAND FOOT SOLDIER

HESSIANS

About 30,000 tough, highly-trained German troops were paid to fight for the British, who couldn't raise enough troops at home. (Most of Britain's money filled the pockets of a German prince who had sold the men's services. The soldiers themselves were poorly paid.)

GRENADIER • FIELD YAGER CORPS • DRAGOON

LOYALISTS (ALSO CALLED TORIES)

About one of every five American soldiers fought alongside British troops or acted as their guides or spies. Most were honorable people who risked their lives for the crown. Most (but not all) came from the privileged classes. Others were black slaves who hoped to gain their freedom by joining the army.

NEW YORK BRIGADE WINTER UNIFORM • NEW YORK BRIGADE SUMMER UNIFORM • RANGER

INDIANS

A majority of Native Americans in the war fought for Great Britain, mainly because they didn't want the colonists to take away their land.

JOSEPH BRANT
MOHAWK CHIEF

CORN PLANTER
SENECA CHIEF

RED JACKET
SENECA ORATOR

BRITISH NAVY

Considered the world's finest naval force, its 468 war vessels and transports moved almost unopposed up and down the east coast of North America to deliver fresh military supplies and food from England to British troops.

In Europe, soldiers were taught that the fair and honorable way to fight was to march openly into battle in columns, line up in rows shoulder to shoulder, and advance toward the enemy without firing a shot until they were close enough to be sure of hitting their targets. Since their muskets were not very accurate, they fired together all at once. Troops were traditionally trained to fight on flat land during the daytime in good weather. Nothing had prepared them to fight their way through thick forests, raging rivers, mosquito-infested swamps, and long mountain ranges.

Rebel Forces

George Washington took command of the Continental Army, the colonies' main fighting force, on July 3, 1775, in Cambridge, Massachusetts. He immediately took steps to build a professional army. It wouldn't be easy. Washington despaired over the inexperience of his volunteers, the constant desertions, and a paralyzing lack of food and military supplies. Sometimes redcoats could shoot rebel soldiers at will because the rebels didn't have enough gunpowder to shoot back. There were three types of forces fighting against the British.

GEORGE WASHINGTON'S CONTINENTAL ARMY

Most men in this volunteer army were private citizens who had signed on for a year or less. The great majority brought their own weapons, food, and clothing. Some colonels bought uniforms for their regiments, but most soldiers never owned one. They wore hunting shirts instead. Compared to their opponents, the men had little training, and even less pay. Though the soldiers were promised money and land for their services, the Continental Congress rarely paid on time, if at all. Sometimes there were as many soldiers who deserted each day as there were men who signed up to fight. To fill their ranks, rebel forces began accepting free blacks and later accepted slaves. By the war's end, some estimated that about one-quarter of the Continental Army was black. The Army also got a tremendous boost from foreign volunteers, including experienced, quick-witted leaders from France, Germany, and Poland.

A handful of Washington's highest-ranking officers were brilliant leaders, but many were unfit for office and looted, sold army blankets, and disobeyed orders. The officers included a Boston bookseller, a breeches maker, a horse dealer, a hat maker, an innkeeper, a blacksmith, an English corporal who had deserted, a preacher, a butcher, a farmer, a farmhand, a tanner's hand, a swineherd, and a dancing teacher.

GENERAL

RHODE ISLAND ARTILLERY OFFICER

MASSACHUSETTS ARTILLERY OFFICER

GREEN MOUNTAIN RANGER

MARYLAND STATE TROOPS

CANADIAN LIGHT INFANTRY

MOYLAND'S LIGHT DRAGOON

NEW YORK CONTINENTAL LINE

CONNECTICUT LIGHT HORSE MILITIA

GEORGIA INFANTRY

MARYLAND INFANTRY

FRENCH INFANTRY

CONTINENTAL NAVY

A feisty infant Navy defended the coast. At its height, it had only 57 ships. The Navy couldn't hope to challenge the huge British warships, so it tried its best to damage British trade and capture or destroy enemy vessels. The Americans also had a trick up their sleeves. They were getting extra help from as many as 1,697 privately owned armed vessels. These privateers preyed upon enemy merchant ships. George Washington was part owner of at least one of them.

LIEUTENANT · ORDINARY SEAMAN · COMMODORE

MILITIAS

Since long before the Revolutionary War, many local areas and every colony except Pennsylvania had raised separate armed forces called militias to defend their communities from attack. Most of these soldiers had even less training than the men in the Continental Army, and their record was mixed. But militias played a crucial role in every one of Washington's victories, and they were very effective in some other important battles as well. This was partly because their style of fighting was new to their enemies, but it was mostly because they could raise enormous numbers of men on short notice and outnumber their opponents.

RANGERS & FRONTIERSMEN · RIFLEMAN · CONNECTICUT FOOT GUARD

In the open field the rebels do not count for much, but in the woods they are formidable. They lie like bacon hunters...and slip from one tree to the other.

HESSIAN SOLDIER

As difficult as things were for the rebel forces, they did have some strong advantages. Though George Washington drilled his army in British-style warfare, rebel soldiers had learned from fighting the Indians to travel light, hide in the woods and mountains, and use ambushes and lightning raids against an unsuspecting enemy. They could move quickly, and their earth-toned homespun and buckskin clothes let them melt into the countryside unseen. The British considered these tactics to be dishonorable.

A New Nation
1776

While Washington's soldiers and King George's soldiers were fighting one another, the Continental Congress made a crucial decision. Instead of just battlling for their rights as citizens of Great Britain, they decided to aim for total American independence.

To rally Americans to their cause and get support from Europe, they set to work writing a document that claimed the right of all people to choose their own government. It also placed the blame for every single one of their grievances squarely on the shoulders of King George himself.

This document was the Declaration of Independence, and its signers had just given birth to the United States of America. In modern language, here are some of the points it made about independence and just a few of the things it said about King George (even though it was really Great Britain's Parliament that had made all the laws oppressing the colonies).

All men are created equal.

They have the right to life, liberty, and happiness.

The Colonies should be free from Great Britain.

- King George won't approve laws made by the colonists.
- He won't allow colonial governing bodies to have meetings.
- He won't let the colonists settle in western lands.
- He makes our citizens feed and house his soldiers for free even during peacetime and won't punish them even if they commit murder.
- He won't let us trade our goods with other countries.

- He taxes us without our consent.
- He won't let us have fair trials by jury.
- He has stolen our ships, wrecked our land, burned our houses, and ruined our businesses.
- He is sending cruel armies to destroy us.
- When he captures our citizens at sea, they must either fight against their own countrymen or kill themselves.
- He encourages our slaves and the merciless Indian Savages to fight against us.

"A prince, whose character is thus marked by every act which may define a tyrant," it stated, "is unfit to be the ruler of a free people."

Supporters of Great Britain thought the signers were traitors who used the Declaration of Independence to attack their own king and promote war against him. To American rebels, though, King George was a traitor to his own British citizens in America because he refused to uphold their British constitutional rights. The rebels gathered to celebrate their independence. Tremendous crowds of merrymakers beat drums, burned bonfires, held a mock burial of King George, and pulled a gilded statue of the king on horseback off its pedestal and melted it down to make bullets for army muskets. The king was thoroughly dismayed.

The Tides of War
1776–1783

The Declaration of Independence may have sounded great to American rebels, but George Washington's army was getting trounced.

I think I shall soon hear...loyal subjects, returning to that duty they owe to an indulgent sovereign.

KING GEORGE

It was Christmas 1776, and the weather was bitter cold. A well-equipped army of 1,400 British-backed Hessian troops was encamped in Trenton, New Jersey, where their commander was sleeping off a holiday feast.

George Washington and his dejected volunteer army of about 6,000 sick, starving, and mostly barefooted rebels had little to celebrate. They had been on the run all the way from New York through New Jersey, finally reaching Pennsylvania, where they camped across the Delaware River from the enemy. In just one week, about half of these men were due to leave for home when their enlistment time ran out.

I am wearied almost to death. I think the game is pretty near up.

GEORGE WASHINGTON

Desperate for a victory, Washington had decided to chance a surprise attack on the Hessians. Along with about 2,400 soldiers who were strong enough to fight, he spent an entire afternoon and night crossing the ice-choked Delaware River in blinding sleet and snow.

They covered their muskets with blankets to keep them dry and marched nine miles toward Trenton in "profound silence."

Washington's men ambushed the sleeping Hessians, who were taken completely by surprise. The disorganized Hessian commander and 150 of his men were killed. The Continental Army captured well over 900 Hessians, and not a single American died in the battle.

As soon as he heard that Washington had clobbered the Hessians, British General Charles Lord Cornwallis sent another 8,000 men to

Trenton to teach the rebels a lesson. Washington and his outnumbered but spirited troops went on to win the Second Battle of Trenton on January 2, 1777, and they won again at Princeton the very next day. In just ten days, Washington's victories had turned the entire war around. Now both sides knew that the Americans had a real army and a chance of winning the war. Many men who were about to leave for home signed on to fight again.

Background scene shows the First Battle of Trenton.
In the foreground, Washington leads his troops at the Battle of Princeton.

That September, British troops aided by American loyalists outfoxed Washington at Brandywine Creek. About 1,400 of his men were killed, wounded, or taken prisoner. Plundering all the farms in their path, British forces headed straight for Philadelphia, America's capital city. The Continental Congress fled in great confusion, and the British Army paraded joyfully into the city without firing a shot. In a fierce battle on October 4, Washington was narrowly defeated at Germantown and lost his chance to retake Philadelphia. Once again, it looked like the rebel army would never beat the British. King George was thrilled.

Meanwhile, in northern New York, another rebel force led by Horatio Gates and Benedict Arnold was having better luck. After a series of battles in September and October 1777, the rebels surrounded British troops at Saratoga and forced their entire army to surrender. It was the biggest blow yet for the Crown and turned the tide of war back in favor of America.

This time the king was agonized when he heard the news. To hide his concern, King George tried so hard to make merry in public that he embarrassed all his friends. He paid no attention to anybody who thought the British would lose.

During the winter of 1777 and 1778, large numbers of King George's supporters in England, Scotland, and Wales signed up to go fight against America. At the same time, a noisy debate was raging about whether the war should continue. Members of Parliament who were sympathetic to the rebels even argued that anyone who helped the British war effort was a criminal. In February, a huge crowd of swearing men and tearful women created an uproar outside the Parliament then broke down the doors and stampeded their way in to hear an especially exciting debate.

Back in America, it was too cold to fight. Gangs of Loyalists and civilians pretending to be patriot militia went on a looting and burning spree. Meanwhile, British Major General "Dandy Sir Billy" Howe spent his time wining and dining his troops in warm, comfortable Philadelphia homes. He rode about in an elegant coach attending every ball, play, and cockfight in town.

GENERAL WILLIAM HOWE

Washington and his half naked "army of skeletons" suffered through another freezing winter, this time 18 miles outside of Philadelphia at Valley Forge. There was no money to buy food. Farmers sold their crops and cattle to British troops, who had plenty of money to spend. About 2,500 of Washington's 11,000 men starved, froze to death, or died from smallpox or pneumonia, and many more deserted. Congress didn't pay the Army for weeks and weeks. Frustrated and angry, Washington wrote Congress that his men had "not even the shadow of a blanket."

Their feet and their legs froze until they were black, and it was often necessary to amputate.

MARQUIS DE LAFAYETTE
Volunteer French military officer fighting for the rebels.

Some people thought the Continental Congress should fire General Washington for losing his recent battles and replace him with Horatio Gates, who had won at Saratoga. But Washington wasn't fired. His shoeless men built a thousand crude huts using timber they cut and trimmed themselves. A Prussian volunteer named Baron von Steuben arrived to teach military drills to the men. And with great reluctance, Washington finally sent his starving soldiers to seize livestock and produce from supporters of the Crown.

Wholehearted respect and affection for Washington was so great that for each man who deserted the army, a hundred more stayed until spring to fight for their cause and country. Once there was food to eat, recruits began pouring in. The training was paying off, too. Washington's ragtag soldiers had finally become professionals.

Stand straight and firm...The toes turned out; the belly drawn in...the shoulders square to the front and kept back...

BARON VON STEUBEN

The king's critics in England still howled that the war wasn't worth the cost. People were losing their jobs because Great Britain no longer sold goods to Americans. In London, redcoats killed 500 unemployed workers who were rioting in the streets.

The French greatly admired the American cause. On February 6, 1778, King Louis XVI of France signed a treaty that recognized the United States as a new nation. He promised to send ships, soldiers, and money to help the rebel army fight his old enemy, the British.

All this time, the flames of war raged on. Out on the western frontier, George Rogers Clark led about 170 men on an 18-day march through a flooded river of icy water up to their knees, chests, and necks to capture a British fort at Vincennes in Indian country.

In the North Sea near Britain, American John Paul Jones's old armed merchant ship *Bonhomme Richard* captured the new British warship *Serapis*.

More and more black soldiers were fighting for both sides. In the southern states, some slave owners, too lazy or afraid to fight, sent their slaves to fight instead. A visitor to the mostly black Rhode Island Regiment said it was "the most neatly dressed, the best under arms, and the most precise in its movements."

In May 1780, the patriots lost Charleston, South Carolina, along with 5,500 soldiers and four ships. It was their worst defeat of the war.

So what was happening to American civilians all this time? For one thing, a vicious civil war was being fought between Americans in favor of independence and Americans who were against it. In the north, rebels broke into homes of Americans loyal to King George and hauled them off to prison. Quakers couldn't fight for religious reasons. The patriots tarred and feathered them anyway, even when they hired substitutes. When times got too rough, loyalists fled to the British colonies of Canada and Nova Scotia, where the government gave them money to pay for their losses. Brutality was even worse in the south, where families were ripped apart and neighbors murdered neighbors.

...the evil rages with more violence than ever. If a stop cannot be put to these massacres the country will be depopulated in a few months....

NATHANAEL GREENE

Meanwhile, the redcoats were trying to terrorize rebel supporters into giving up. Besides constantly stealing food and horses, they burned entire towns and villages, looted or seized people's houses, raped and murdered innocent civilians, and set fire to crops and timberland. British troops locked prisoners in filthy prison ships where they died like flies from starvation, heat, cold, and disease.

Indians fighting alongside the British burned almost 1,000 homes, tortured and killed whole families, and scalped the dead. Believing that it would make them more powerful, some Indians honored their bravest victims by eating them.

For revenge, rebel troops sent by George Washington destroyed 41 Native American villages, many of which were peaceful, and burned all their crops and orchards. They collected scalps and showed off pairs of leggings made from the skin of dead Indians. The Iroquois people call George Washington "Town Destroyer" to this very day.

Plenty of women were involved in the war, too. Some of them served as spies or guides. A Quaker housewife living across from British headquarters in Philadelphia often overheard information about redcoat war plans. She sewed the news inside cloth-covered buttons and sent her young son to deliver them to George Washington. A black woman named Quamino Dolly guided British soldiers through a swamp so that they could sneak up behind rebel troops and capture Savannah, Georgia.

Women on both sides regularly traveled with the soldiers, who were often their husbands. Sometimes they even brought along their children. They cooked food, cleaned out the cannons, washed clothes, made bandages, knit socks, nursed the sick, and laid out the dead. When there was no fighting, they danced and sang with the soldiers, but when times got tough, some women fought in battles right alongside the men. George Washington's wife, Martha, spent eight winters with her husband, and she worked just as hard as anyone.

Flirtatious German-speaking women in Pennsylvania lured lots of Hessian soldiers into trading their hard military life for an American wife and farm. And there were often romances between American women and the dashing British soldiers quartered in private homes.

> Of course I had many beaux who flattered me and danced with me, and one who...would have given his eyes for me if I would have taken them.

VIRGINIA WOMAN

Some foreigners applauded the patriots.

> There is more simplicity, cordiality, and courtesy here than in England... The American women are very pretty...

> In America there are no poor, nor even what we call peasantry. Each individual has...the same rights as the most wealthy landed proprietor.

MARQUIS DE LAFAYETTE

Others disagreed.

> The spirit of rebellion is not yet weary of forcing the inhabitants to [take up] arms by flattery, deception, threats, and open violence...

GERMAN OFFICER IN NEW YORK

> At first I was inclined to be favorable to the Americans. But since I have had a chance to get closer with their history, motives, and character, I have no further wishes for them.

The Final Battle

Leaders on both sides began to think the war could finally be won with a major victory in the south. Up north in New York, George Washington got wind that British General Charles Lord Cornwallis and his men were marching toward the Virginia tobacco port city of Yorktown on the Chesapeake Bay, brutally terrorizing area residents as they went. In August 1781, Cornwallis finished setting up his base of operations.

Washington had just learned that the French were sending 28 ships to help the American forces. Would it be possible to set a trap for Cornwallis? The timing would have to be absolutely perfect. First, Washington's men joined forces with an army of French ground troops in New York. Then both armies sneaked past the northern redcoats and raced night and day for 500 miles all the way south toward Yorktown.

Meanwhile, the 28 French ships sailed into the mouth of the long Chesapeake Bay. This news was sent by courier to George Washington, whose men had just reached the top of the Bay. Famous for being calm and dignified, Washington was so excited that he jumped up and down and waved his hat with glee. The trap could now be set!

But before long, cannon fire boomed across the water. Great Britain's Navy had arrived, too, and was fighting the French. Just in time, the French ships whipped Great Britain's Navy and sent them packing!

Now Cornwallis couldn't escape by water. By early October, Washington's troops and the French Army and Navy had joined to surround him.

Cornwallis was outnumbered two to one, but he hadn't given up hope. He had sent word to the British generals up in New York pleading for help, and he expected it to arrive at any moment. Not a chance. Commander-in-Chief Sir Henry Clinton kept making excuses not to fight. Besides, he was too busy entertaining a visitor—King George's young son, Prince William, who thought he might like to become the Royal Governor of Virginia.

By October 17, three weeks after Washington set the trap, Cornwallis's forces were starving. Unburied bodies lay everywhere, the ground was shaking violently from the thunder of a hundred cannons, and the sky was streaked with red from shots flying across enemy lines. All of a sudden a British officer appeared through the smoke waving a white handkerchief to signal defeat. Joyous American forces started to let out a tremendous cheer, but George Washington silenced his men, shouting, "Let history huzzah for you."

Claiming he was sick, General Cornwallis snubbed George Washington by sending his second-in-command to surrender his sword to a French commander who had fought alongside the Americans. The Frenchman turned the British officer away by pointing toward General Washington, the real commanding officer. Washington pointed Cornwallis's second-in-command toward his own second-in-command, and when the British sword was at last surrendered, the Revolutionary War was unofficially over.

No Kings for America

King George tried hard to continue the struggle, but British support faded fast. The king was so humiliated that he almost gave up his crown. It took several years for his attitude to change.

> Till driven to the wall I certainly will do what I can to save the Empire; and if I do not succeed, I will... not be a tool in the destruction of the honor of the country.

KING GEORGE III

George Washington was encouraged by an officer in his army to become the king of America. He was horrified.

> If you have any regard for your Country, concern for yourself or posterity, or respect for me, banish these thoughts from your mind.

GEORGE WASHINGTON

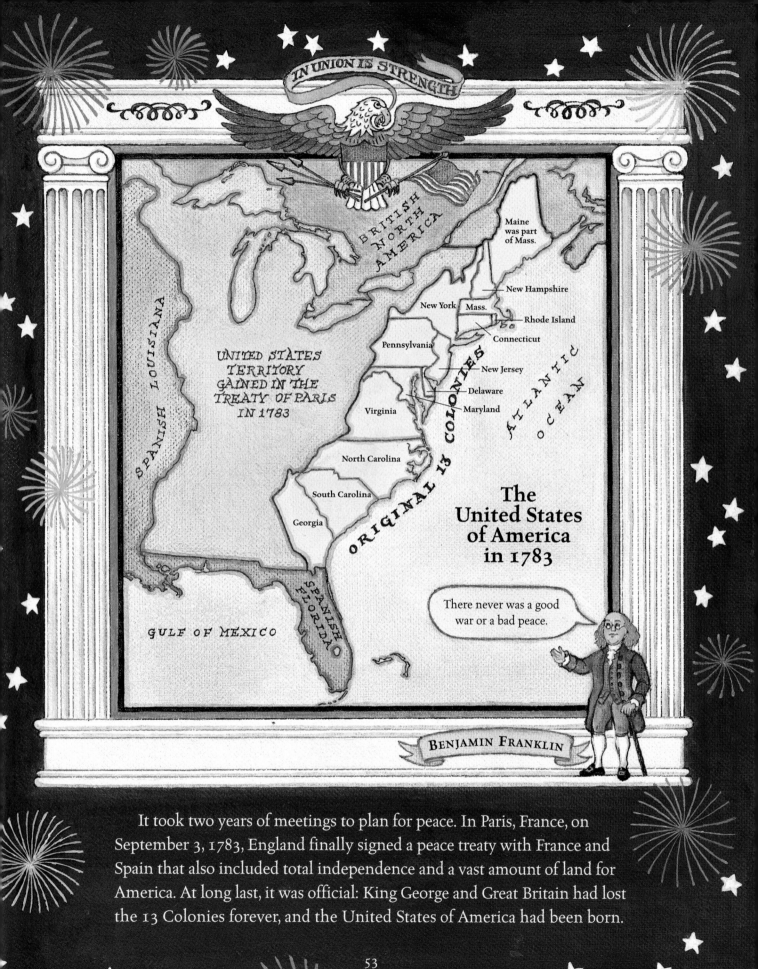

It took two years of meetings to plan for peace. In Paris, France, on September 3, 1783, England finally signed a peace treaty with France and Spain that also included total independence and a vast amount of land for America. At long last, it was official: King George and Great Britain had lost the 13 Colonies forever, and the United States of America had been born.

> I wished some of my violent Countrymen could have had such an opportunity as I have had. I think that they would be convinced that George the Third has not one grain of Tyranny...and that he cannot be that bloody-minded man they have so repeatedly called him. It is impossible; a man of his fine feelings, so good a husband, so kind a Father, cannot be a Tyrant.
>
> SAMUEL SHOEMAKER
> American Loyalist who met
> King George in 1784

What Ever Happened to King George III?

The last king of America was no villain, but to this very day, some people believe he was an insane, dim-witted tyrant. Many Americans blame him personally for every British act of repression. But the truth is that King George was Great Britain's most cultured monarch and was filled with good intentions.

Like all other kings and most Europeans at the time, he believed that God granted kings and nobility the divine right to rule. He considered it his religious and patriotic duty to uphold age-old British rights and liberties and the duty of his subjects to respect the Crown by obeying British law.

King George sincerely wished to be a good father to *all* his people, including Americans. "I do not pretend to any superior abilities," he once said, "but will give place to no man in meaning to preserve... freedom, happiness, and glory. That I have erred is undoubted, otherwise I should not be human, but...wherever I have failed, it has been from the head not the heart."

The king was sure his loss of America would make Britain a second-rate power. It didn't. King George, Parliament, and the young United States all needed each other. John Adams traveled from America in 1785 to meet with King George and try to restore good relations.

"I will be very frank with you," the king told him. "I was the last to consent to the separation; but...I have always said...that I would be the first to meet the friendship of the United States as an independent power." Before long, Great Britain was making more money trading with an independent America than it had ever made from dealing with the Colonies.

During King George's reign, the Industrial Revolution helped to make Britain the world's richest nation. Far-reaching British explorations took place in the Pacific Ocean, near Antarctica, and on the continent of Africa.

The king practiced scientific farming, had a powerful telescope built, and collected scientific instruments. Music flourished. King George began a Royal Academy of Arts. This generous monarch freely opened his excellent library to scholars, gave an enormous amount of his own money to charities and the needy, and improved education for the poor.

Even so, his popularity swung up and down. At times he was viciously mocked in cartoons, and there were several attempts to assassinate him. By 1809, though, almost everyone in England seemed to love him and to admire his moral character. Following a Jubilee celebrating a British victory in yet another war with France, one newspaper reported that "The whole nation was like one great family in thanksgiving for the Father of the People."

Perhaps as early as 1765, King George began to suffer brief bouts of madness caused by a rare hereditary disease now known as porphyria. Between 1810 and the time of his death, he became blind, almost deaf, and increasingly more insane, stamping violently, allowing no one to cut his wild white beard, and holding long conversations with angels. Every so often, he seemed to be getting better. At other times, though, his doctors confined him in a straitjacket. In his old age, he said "I that am born a gentleman shall never rest my head on my last pillow in peace and quiet as long as I remember the loss of my American colonies."

In 1811 when King George became too ill to rule, his son, the Prince of Wales, was sworn in as Regent. The king finally died at age 82 in 1820. Over 30,000 black-clad mourners attended his funeral. One of these remarked, "thus sunk into an honored grave the best man and best king that ever adorned humanity, and who...for sixty long years had been a father to his people."

He was, in every sense of the words, a wise, a good, and a great man. He was incapable of fear, meeting personal dangers with the calmest unconcern. His integrity was most pure, his justice, inflexible, the whole of his character was in its mass perfect.

THOMAS JEFFERSON
Third President of the United States

What Did George Washington Do Next?

By the end of the Revolutionary War, George Washington was more than a war hero; he was the most beloved and admired person in America. In May 1787, he was unanimously chosen to be president of the Constitutional Convention, whose members were writing the Constitution of the United States. Under his fair, quiet leadership, it went into effect a year later. It has been called the greatest document of its kind ever written.

The Continental Congress ran the new country for six years until February 1789, when George Washington was elected by the members of the Electoral College in each state to become the first President of the United States. Washington, now 57 years old, was worried about his ability to lead this experiment in governing the nation. "My movements to the chair of government will be accompanied by feelings not unlike those of a culprit, who is going to the place of his execution," he said. He feared there would be "an ocean of difficulties."

The night before his inauguration on April 30, New York City overflowed with people vowing they would sleep in tents if necessary to get a look at their champion. Thousands cheered and women tossed flower petals. Cannons boomed. There were glorious parades and emotional speeches. George Washington was determined not to become his Majesty the King of America, but simply Mr. President. He wore a plain brown suit, simple black shoes with silver buckles, plain white silk stockings, and a long sword with a silver handle, all made in America.

Washington served two full terms in office with such dignity

and honor that he became the role model for all future American Presidents. Five new states joined the union while he was in office. The Constitutional amendments in the Bill of Rights were approved by the states. And Washington worked hard to keep his young nation out of yet another war between Great Britain and France.

Refusing to run for a third term as President, he returned with delight to his beloved Mount Vernon in March 1797. "I can truly say I had rather be at home at Mount Vernon with a friend or two about me than to be attended at the seat of government by the officers of state and the representatives of every power in Europe," he wrote.

Even in retirement, though, he kept up with world events by subscribing to ten newspapers, and visitors stopped by constantly to ask his opinions about policy. He once told a visiting English actor that owning slaves made him miserable and threatened his life's work. "I can clearly foresee that nothing but the rooting out of slavery can [save] our nation," he lamented.

Less than three years after leaving the presidency, Washington caught a severe chill while inspecting his fields in the sleet and rain. Though he had been in good health, he died within three days on December 14, 1799, at the age of 67. His passing marked the end of the century and the end of an era.

Later that month, Congress adopted a document written by General Henry "Light-Horse Harry" Lee proclaiming George Washington as "first in war, first in peace, and first in the hearts of his countrymen." George Washington had earned his place in history as the father of his country.

Acknowledgments

When George Washington was selected to head the Continental Army, he said "I do not think myself equal to the Command." That's exactly how I felt when I began to work on this story. Writing and illustrating this book was the most difficult task I have ever tackled—and one of the most rewarding.

My mission was to cram 20 years of history, biography, and philosophy into a picture book that kids could grasp and enjoy. I strove to paint accurate likenesses of all 22 historical figures quoted in the book (and make them look the age they were at the time); to correctly portray everything else, from clothing, uniforms, and scenery to weapons, boats, and architecture; and to decide which of the many versions of history I found seemed closest to the truth.

I would like to thank many people for trying to insure that I got the facts straight and for helping to keep me honest. Any mistakes I have made are solely my own.

My terrific editor, Nancy Laties Feresten, encouraged me to take on this project and waded through many thick stacks of manuscripts with patience and enthusiasm.

Special thanks are due to Linda Grant De Pauw, Ph.D., Professor Emeritus in History at George Washington University, founder of the MINERVA Center for the study of women and the military, and author of *Founding Mothers*, for her thoughtful commentaries and thorough review of both text and art. Peter Reaveley, an expert on John Paul Jones's battle at sea, kindly sent me innumerable pictures of the ships as seen from every angle. I also received excellent

suggestions from William Deary, Ph.D., who lectures about the war from the British point of view, and his wife, Mary Ann Deary, who formerly worked at Mount Vernon and is an expert on George and Martha Washington.

Kate Ray, a student at the Sidwell Friends School in Washington, D.C., made some great comments about the text from a student's point of view. Teacher Monica Edinger from the Dalton School in New York City helped to ensure that the events and vocabulary in my story would be easily understood by this age group.

Thanks also to my graphic designer, David Seager, and to National Geographic's map expert Carl Mehler, for their generous aid and support.

Bibliography

I consulted hundreds of sources in my research for the text and the artwork for this book. Many of my paintings are loosely based on period paintings, etchings, and cartoons. Here is a selection of sources that were most valuable to me.

Books:

American Heritage, eds. *The American Heritage Book of the Presidents and Famous Americans*, Volume 1. New York: Dell Publishing Company, 1967.

Andrist, Ralph K., ed. *George Washington: A Biography in His Own Words*, Volume 1. New York: Newsweek, 1972.

Bober, Natalie S. *Countdown to Independence: A Revolution of Ideas in England and Her American Colonies: 1760–1776*. New York: Atheneum Books for Young Readers, 2001.

Brand, Oscar. *Songs of '76: A Folksinger's History of the Revolution*. New York: M. Evans and Company, 1972.

Brands, H.W. *The First American: The Life and Times of Benjamin Franklin*. New York: Doubleday, 2000.

Brooke, John. *King George III*. London: Constable, 1992.

English, William Hayden, ed. *Conquest of the Country Northwest of the River Ohio 1778–1783 and Life of Gen. George Rogers Clark*. Indianapolis, IN: Bowen-Merril Company, 1897.

Fleming, Thomas J. *First in Their Hearts: A Biography of George Washington*. New York: Walker and Company, 1967.

Hibbert, Christopher. *George III: A Personal History*. New York: Basic Books, 1998.

—. *Redcoats and Rebels: The American Revolution Through British Eyes*. New York: Norton, 1990.

Jefferson, Thomas. *The Writings of Thomas Jefferson* (ed., Paul Leicester Ford). New York: Putnam, 1892–99.

Kent, Zachary. *George Washington: First President of the United States*. Chicago: Children's Press, 1986.

Leckie, Robert. *George Washington's War: The Saga of the American Revolution*. New York: HarperCollins, 1992.

Lefferts, Lt. Charles M. *Uniforms of the Armies in the War of the American Revolution*. New York: New York Historical Society, 1926.

Lloyd, Alan. *The King Who Lost America: A Portrait of the Life and Times of George III*. Garden City, NY: Doubleday and Company, Inc., 1971.

Marrin, Albert. *The War for Independence: The Story of the American Revolution*. Fairfield, PA: Atheneum Books for Young Readers, 1988.

—. *George Washington and the Founding of a Nation*. New York: Dutton Children's Books, 2001.

Morris, Richard B. and editors, Time-Life Books. *The Life History of the United States: The New World/Before 1775*. New York: Time-Life Books, 1963, revised 1974.

—. *The Life History of the United States: The Making of a Nation/1775–1789*. New York: Time-Life Books, 1963, revised 1974.

Pearson, Kenneth and Conner, Patricia. *1776: The British Story of the American Revolution*. London: Times Newspapers Ltd., 1976.

Pearson, Michael. *Those Yankee Rebels: Being the True and Amazing History of the American Revolution as Seen through British Eyes*. New York: Putnam, 1974.

Pettengill, Ray W., ed. *Letters from America 1776–1779: Being Letters of Brunswick, Hessian, and Waldeck Officers with the British Armies During the Revolution*. Port Washington, NY: Kennikat Press, 1924.

Rhodehamel, John, ed. *Washington: Writings*. New York: The Library of America, 1997.

Rosenburg, John. *First in War: George Washington in the American Revolution.* Brookfield, CT: Millbrook Press, 1998.

Seymour, Peter, ed. *The Spirit of 1776: Life, Liberty and the Pursuit of Happiness During the American Revolution.* Kansas City, Missouri: Hallmark Editions, 1971.

Shroeder, John Frederick, ed. *Maxims of George Washington: Political, Military, Social, Moral, and Religious.* Mount Vernon, VA: The Mount Vernon Ladies' Association, 1989.

Time-Life Books, eds. *Winds of Revolution: TimeFrame AD 1700–1800.* Alexandria, VA: Time-Life Books, 1990.

Thomas Evan. *John Paul Jones: Sailor, Hero, Father of the American Navy.* New York: Simon & Schuster, 2003.

Tuchman, Barbara W. *The First Salute.* New York: Knopf, 1988.

Washington, George. *Writings.* New York: Library of America, 1997.

Washington, George. *The Writings of George Washington.* Washington, DC: U.S. Government Printing Office, 1939

Web sites:

Department of the Navy—Navy Historical Center. "Vessels of the Continental Navy." www.history.navy.mil/wars/revwar/contships.htm.

PBS Online and KTCA's The Tube. "Chronicle of the Revolution," *Liberty!: The American Revolution:* www.pbs.org/ktca/liberty/chronicle.

Ten Crucial Days: Commemorating the Crossing of the Delaware and the Battles of Trenton and Princeton: www.tencrucialdays.com.

Selig, Robert A. "The Revolution's Black Soldiers." www.americanrevolution.org/blk.html.

The George Washington Papers at the Library of Congress 1741-1799: memory.loc.gov/ammem/gwhtml/gwhome.html.

"Uniforms of the American Revolution": www.srcalifornia.com/sr3.htm.

Quote Sources

Sources in parentheses refer to entries in Bibliography.

p. 7, "Royal brute..." (Thomas Paine, *Common Sense*); "the Father of the People..." (Hibbert, *George III*, 392); p. 8, Indian Chief: "Mark yon tall..." (Fleming, 48-49); p. 9, Samuel Johnson: "Of him..." (Hibbert, *George III*, 79); p. 18, Samuel Adams: "If our trade.." (Bober, 43); anonymous English poet: "This stamp act..." (Lloyd, 185); p. 19, anonymous note: "What greater joy..." (Hibbert, *Redcoats and Rebels*, 3); King George: "I am more..." (Lloyd, 186); p. 20, Charles Townshend: "I dare tax..." (Bober, 115); p. 22, King George: "gentlemen who pretend..." (Hibbert, *George III*, 142); three youths: "Fire! By God!...," "You coward...," "You can't kill.." (Hibbert, *Redcoats and Rebels*, 13-14); p. 23, King George: "There must always..." (Hibbert, *Redcoats and Rebels*, 18); "force it on shore..." (said by participant George Hewes, Seymour, 6); p. 24–25, "Boston harbor..." (Bober, 189); "Tea is the..." (Hibbert, *Redcoats and Rebels*, 19); "Rally Mohawks..." (Bober, 191)Samuel Johnson: "a race of convicts..." (Pearson & Conner, 67); p. 26, George Washington: "I am ready..." (Fleming, 52); p. 27, Thomas Gage: "Affairs here..." (Hibbert, *Redcoats and Rebels*, 27); Patrick Henry: "Our chains are forged..." (www.libertyonline.hypermall.com); Charles Van: "You will never..." (Hibbert, *Redcoats and Rebels*, 24); Samuel Johnson: "How is it..." (pamphlet "Taxation no Tyranny," March 1775); King George: "The New England..."

(Brooke, 175); p. 28, John Pitcairn: "Lay down your..." (Hibbert, *Redcoats and Rebels*, 32); p. 29, Major Buttrick: "Fire, fellow soldiers..." (Hibbert, *Redcoats and Rebels*, 33); Dr. Joseph Warren: "These fellows say..." (Morris, 1775–1789, 9); George Washington: "A brother's sword..." (Washington, 164); p. 30, George Washington: "I do not..." (Andrist, 101); p. 31, Israel Putnam: "Don't fire until..." (Leckie, 159); William Howe: "From and absurd..." (Leckie, 166); Henry Clinton: "A dear-bought victory..." (Leckie, 164); Thomas Gage: "These people show..." (Leckie 165–6); p. 35, Hessian soldier: "In the open..." (Pettengill, 80); p. 37, John Hancock: "There, I guess..." (Leckie, 256); Ben Franklin: "We must indeed..." (Leckie, p. 256); Benjamin Harrison: "I shall have..." (www.rebelswithavision.com); King George: "I wish nothing..." (Lloyn, 212); p. 38, King George: "I think I..." (Lloyd, 240); George Washington: "I am wearied..." (American Heritage, 17); p. 41, George Washington: "It's a fine..." (American Heritage, 34); p. 42, King George: "I have beat..." (Lloyd, 244); p. 43, William Pitt: "You cannot conquer..." (Lloyd, 243–244); p. 45, Marquis de Lafayette: "Their feet and..." (McCombs, Phil. "Their Humbling Sacrifice," *The Washington Post*, 2/25/02, C10); Baron Von Steuben: "Stand straight and..." (Rosenburg, 149); p. 46, George Rogers Clark: "The ice, in..." and "I...caused the..." (English, part 7, Feb. 17, 1779 and Feb. 23, 1779); p. 47, Richard Pearson: "Have you struck..." (Web site: Department of the

Navy); John Paul Jones: "Struck, sir.." (Seymour, p. 47)(Note: There is much controversy about the exact wording for this quote.); visitor: "the most neatly..." (Marrin, 188); Nathanael Greene: "We fight, we..." (Marrin, 251); p. 48, Nathanael Greene: "the evil rages..." (Brand, 90); p. 49, Virginia woman: "Of course I..." (Seymour, 34); Marquis de Lafayette: "There is more..." (Seymour, 38-39); German officer: "The spirit of..." (Pettingill, 228–229); p. 51, George Washington: "Let history huzzah..." (Web site: PBS Online); p. 52, King George: "Till driven to.." (Lloyd, 273); George Washington: "If you have..." (Fleming, 101); p. 53, Benjamin Franklin: "There never was..." (Brands, 620); p. 54, Samuel Shoemaker: "I wished some..." (Pearson & Conner, 81); King George: "I do not..." (Pearson and Connor, 80); King George: "I will be..." (Hibbert, *George III*, 168); p. 55, "The whole nation..." (Hibbert, *George III*, 392); King George: "I that am born..." (www.dreamscape.com); "Thus sunk to..." (Hibbert, *George III*, 409); p. 56–57, Thomas Jefferson: "He was, in..." (Jefferson, vol. 9, 448); George Washington: "My movements to.." (American Heritage, 21); George Washington: "an ocean of.." (American Heritage, 44); George Washington: "I can truly..." (Washington, *Writings of*, vol 31, 54); George Washington: "I can clearly..." (Marrin, *George Washington and the Founding of a Nation*, 252); Henry "Light-Horse Harry" Lee: "First in war..." (Shroeder, 196).

Index